HUNGARY

By Sloane Gould and
Joanne Mattern

EXPLORING WORLD CULTURES

Cavendish Square

Published in 2026 by Cavendish Square Publishing, LLC
2544 Clinton Street, Buffalo, NY 14224

Second Edition

Library of Congress Cataloging-in-Publication Data

Names: Gould, Sloane, author. | Mattern, Joanne, author.
Title: Hungary / by Sloane Gould and Joanne Mattern
Description: Second edition. | New York : Cavendish Square Publishing, [2026] | Series: Exploring world cultures | Includes index.
Identifiers: LCCN 2024040282 (print) | LCCN 2024040283 (ebook) | ISBN 9781502673398 (library binding) | ISBN 9781502673381 (paperback) | ISBN 9781502673404 (ebook)
Subjects: LCSH: Hungary--Juvenile literature.
Classification: LCC DB906 .G68 2026 (print) | LCC DB906 (ebook) | DDC 943.9--dc23/eng/20241118
LC record available at https://lccn.loc.gov/2024040282
LC ebook record available at https://lccn.loc.gov/2024040283

Writers: Joanne Mattern; Sloane Gould (second edition)
Editor: Caitie McAneney
Copyeditor: Jill Keppeler
Designer: Deanna Lepovich

The photographs in this book are used by permission and through the courtesy of: Cover Jane Biriukova/Shutterstock.com; p. 4 Globe Turner/Shutterstock.com; p. 5 TTstudio/Shutterstock.com; p. 7 (top) Tainar/Shutterstock.com; p. 7 (bottom) kaiser-v/Shutterstock.com; p. 8 Jonas Muscat/Shutterstock.com; p. 9 V_E/Shutterstock.com; p. 10 Savvapanf Photo/Shutterstock.com; p. 11 EM_photo/Shutterstock.com; p. 12 Andrzej Rostek/Shutterstock.com; p. 13 eldar nurkovic/Shutterstock.com; p. 14 Travel Stock/Shutterstock.com; p. 15 Tito Slack/Shutterstock.com; p. 17 (top) belizar/Shutterstock.com; p. 17 (bottom) Ordasiphoto/Shutterstock.com; pp. 18, 26 csikiphoto/Shutterstock.com; p. 19 Mistervlad/Shutterstock.com; p. 20 feelthedrone/Shutterstock.com; p. 21 Kurka Geza Corey/Shutterstock.com; p. 22 Ajdin Kamber/Shutterstock.com; p. 23 vali.lung/Shutterstock.com; p. 24 Matyas Rehak/Shutterstock.com; p. 25 krstrbrt/Shutterstock.com; p. 27 gd_project/Shutterstock.com; p. 28 Pucs Fongabe/Shutterstock.com; p. 29 Mehes Daniel/Shutterstock.com.

CPSIA compliance information: Batch #CS26CSQ: For further information contact Cavendish Square Publishing LLC at 1-877-980-4450.

Printed in the United States of America

CONTENTS

INTRODUCTION

Hungary is a central European country with longstanding **traditions** and a rich **culture**. From the busy city of Budapest to the large farms of the countryside, Hungary has a **diverse** landscape and lifestyles. Hungary has lakes, mountains, and rivers. It's home to the Danube River, which goes through more countries than any other river on Earth. Hungary is a landlocked nation, which means it has no coastline.

This map shows where Hungary is located in central Europe.

Hungary has a long tradition of folk music and stories. Hungarians are known for their folk art and beautiful churches. People in Hungary are hardworking but also like to relax in hot springs. Public spas are a popular place to visit, with a long history. Natural hot springs are just one of the gifts of the nation's geography.

Hungary is home to the Magyar people, who have lived there for around 1,200 years. In that time, Hungarians have built a nation with a strong culture. Let's explore Hungary!

The capital city of Hungary is Budapest.

GEOGRAPHY

Hungary has many central and eastern European neighbors. Austria and Slovenia neighbor Hungary to the west. Croatia and Serbia lie to the south. Romania is east of Hungary. Ukraine and Slovakia border Hungary to the north.

The most important waterway in Hungary is the Danube River. It flows through the middle of Budapest, Hungary's capital city. Budapest was once two separate cities named Buda and Pest. They became one city in 1873.There are mountains in the north and west. In the southeast, the Great Hungarian Plain stretches across almost half of the country. It is covered with grass and provides good land for farming. An area called Transdanubia is in the west. It has many hills.

There are hundreds of caves underneath northwestern Hungary. These caves are part of Aggtelek National Park.

FACT!

Hungary covers 35,919 square miles (93,030 sq km).

Thousands of people visit the caves at Aggtelek National Park every year.

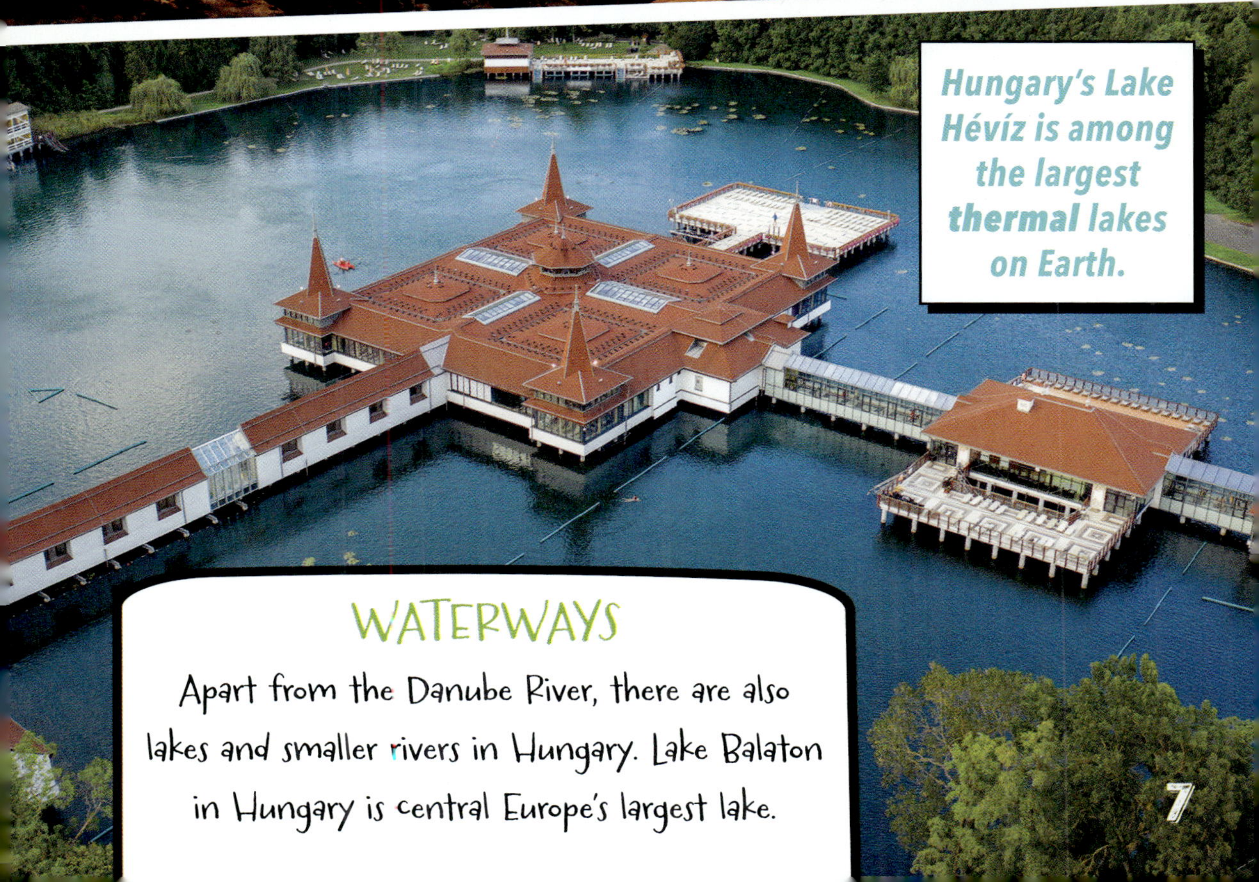

Hungary's Lake Hévíz is among the largest **thermal** lakes on Earth.

WATERWAYS

Apart from the Danube River, there are also lakes and smaller rivers in Hungary. Lake Balaton in Hungary is central Europe's largest lake.

HISTORY

The Magyars have a long history in the area that's now Hungary, dating back to at least the 800s CE. The group of tribes had a leader named Árpád, who is called the founder of Hungary. The country was tested in the 1200s when Mongol warriors came to conquer the area, and again when the Ottoman Empire took over in the 1500s.

Many Ottoman reminders remain in Budapest. This is the resting place of Ottoman poet Gül Baba.

THE OTTOMON EMPIRE

The Ottomon Turks ruled Hungary from 1541 to 1699. This empire controlled much of the Middle East and eastern Europe for 600 years!

During the 1800s, Hungary and Austria joined to form the empire of Austria-Hungary. This empire was destroyed during World War I (1914-1918). After the war, Hungary had to give up much of its land.

After World War II (1939-1945), Hungary became a **Communist** country. Its government was supported by the Soviet Union. In 1989, Hungary shifted from a Communist country to a republic, or country with elected leaders.

FACT!

In World War II, Hungary fought against the United States along with Germany, Italy, and Japan.

Many people visit Budapest for its historical* architecture*. This is Old Fisherman Bastion.

GOVERNMENT

Hungary's government meets in the capital of Budapest. People in Hungary have been able to vote for their leaders since 1990, but it is not considered a full democracy anymore.

The government is split into three parts: executive, judicial, and legislative, or lawmaking. The president and the prime minister make up the executive part. The prime minister has the most power. They appoint, or name, people to lead different departments. The prime minister is elected to a four-year term. The judicial branch enforces the law.

Hungary's flag is red, white, and green.

THE TOP COURT

The top court in Hungary is called the Curia. Smaller courts operate under the Curia. The Curia makes sure laws are carried out correctly.

The National Assembly makes up the legislative part. Each member is elected to a four-year term. The assembly has 199 members. Members of the National Assembly make new laws. They can also make decisions about war or other military actions. They meet in the grand National Assembly building in Budapest to work together.

FACT!

Hungary joined with other countries as part of the European Union in 2004.

This is the building in Budapest where the prime minister works.

THE ECONOMY

Hungary trades with many other European nations. Its main trading partners are Germany, Italy, and Romania. An important industry, or kind of business, in Hungary is manufacturing. Hungary's mines produce a mineral called bauxite that is used to make aluminum. Other workers mine coal, oil, and natural gas. Factory workers make paper products, food, and chemicals. Only about 4 percent of Hungary's workers have jobs on farms. Wheat, corn, potatoes, beets, and sunflower seeds are the top crops.

Hungarian money is called the forint. Forints are decorated with pictures of famous Hungarians.

Many of Hungary's workers have jobs in service industries. Some of them work in hotels, restaurants, museums, and banks. Others work in hospitals and schools. **Tourism** is a big part of Hungary's economy. In 2023, around 49 million people visited Hungary from other countries!

FACT!

About 58 percent of Hungary's income is from the services industry.

Hungary is part of the European Union, so many people visit from other European countries.

HUNGARIAN FARMING HISTORY

Farming was once the largest part of Hungary's economy. In the past, farms were owned by the government. Today, farms are owned by Hungarian citizens.

THE ENVIRONMENT

Hungary is home to many plants and animals. Its main habitats include plains, mountains, and water. Major rivers, like the Danube and Tisza, are home to fish, turtles, and beavers. The country's lakes also have these animals. Birds such as ducks, geese, and swans swim there too. Thousands of cranes fly through Hungary every autumn on their way to Africa for the winter.

Herds of deer roam across the plains in Hungary.

FOREST HABITAT

About 20 percent of Hungary is covered with forests. Beech, oak, poplar, and willow trees are the most common.

Eurasian wolves live in Russia and eastern Europe.

FACT!

Hungary has 10 national parks, which help keep its natural beauty alive.

A variety of animals live in Hungary's forests and fields. Hungary is home to more than 150 kinds of butterflies. Some are common in Hungary but rare in other parts of Europe. Large animals like wild boars and red deer live in the forests. Wolves, bears, and jackals live there too. Throughout history, much of Hungary's forests were cut down for farming and communities. Hungary is working on using cleaner energy sources, but many things are still powered by **fossil fuels**, which pollute the surroundings.

THE PEOPLE TODAY

More than 9.8 million people live in Hungary today. Hungary's population has been getting smaller every year. Fewer babies are being born, and many Hungarians are moving to other countries for work.

Most Hungarians are part of the same **ethnic** group. Their ancestors are the Magyars who ruled long ago. They have specific traditions and ways of life. Another ethnic group in Hungary is the Romani, or Roma. Most Roma once traveled the land in horse-drawn wagons. They were nomads. This means they never stayed in one place for long. Today, most Roma have settled in Hungary's towns and cities. The Roma have been treated badly for hundreds of years. Many Hungarians still treat them as outsiders today.

SMALLER ETHNIC GROUPS

There are also small groups of Germans, Serbs, Slovaks, and Romanians in Hungary. Many of these people moved there after World War II to escape the **violence** in their own countries.

Romani people sell things at a marketplace in Hungary.

FACT!

About 84 percent of people living in Hungary are native Hungarians.

These girls wear traditional Hungarian clothing.

LIFESTYLE

The lifestyle in Hungary is different in the city than in the country. Some parts of Hungary are filled with small villages. There, people live in small houses. Many villagers grow vegetables and fruit in large gardens. There is a lot of green space. People from the city may like to visit the countryside on weekends and holidays.

FACT!
The Hungarian capital of Budapest has a population of about 1.8 million people.

Many Hungarians live in apartments in cities.

Hungary has a great system of public transportation. It's easy to travel by bus or tram.

Most Hungarians live in cities or large towns. The capital, Budapest, is also the largest city in Hungary. Other large cities include Debrecen, Pecs, and Gyor.

Hungarian children often start school when they are three years old. They go to primary schools until they are 14. Students learn Hungarian, math, science, and foreign languages. After that, Hungarians go to secondary school. Here, they get ready to go to college or learn a trade. Students must pass a difficult exam to go to college.

WOMEN IN HUNGARY

Hungarian girls and boys often get the same kind of education. About 54 percent of women are in the workforce.

RELIGION

Christianity has a long history in Hungary. It's still the most popular religion, or faith, today. About 30 percent of Hungarians belong to the Roman Catholic Church. Other Hungarian Christians belong to Protestant churches. Many churches in Hungary are large and **ornate**.

FACT!
Many Hungarians celebrate the Christian holidays of Christmas and Easter.

The Esztergom Basilica is the largest church in Hungary.

Judaism is another important religion in Hungary. Before World War II, more than 800,000 Jews lived in Hungary. Around 440,000 Jews were forced out of Hungary during the **Holocaust**, and many were killed. Since then, Hungary has passed new laws to help Jewish people and communities. Today, around 100,000 Jewish people live in Hungary.

Many modern Hungarians do not follow any religion. Though it's mostly a Christian country, people don't have to follow a religion in Hungary. They are free to choose.

This church in Miskolc, Hungary, is made of only wood with traditional wooden carvings.

THE REFORMATION IN HUNGARY

The Reformation was a movement that led to the rise of Protestantism in the 15th century in Europe. However, by the 18th century, Catholicism was back on the rise in Hungary.

LANGUAGE

What language should you speak if you visit Hungary? Many people there speak English or German. Others speak Russian or French. Students can study these languages in school. However, almost everyone in Hungary speaks Hungarian. Most newspapers are written in Hungarian. Children are taught in Hungarian in school.

This sign on the border of Hungary and Romania has the word for "Hungary" in Magyar.

FACT!

The official name of the Hungarian language is Magyar.

Hungarian has 44 letters. There are 14 vowels that can change the meaning of a word depending on how they are pronounced. There are many rules to follow, but word order can be switched to mean different things. Hungarian is not easy to learn. However, some simple things to say include "thank you" and "you're welcome." "Thank you" is *köszönöm* (KUH-suh-num), and "you're welcome" is *szívesen* (SEE-vah-shen).

THE ORIGIN OF MAGYAR

The Magyar language originally came from the area around Finland and Russia, in northern Europe and Asia.

These welcome signs in Hungary are written in Magyar.

ARTS AND FESTIVALS

Folk art has a strong history in Hungary. People enjoy painting flowers, birds, and plants on furniture, plates, and other objects. There are many art museums. The grand architecture of Hungary also reflects its art and history.

Music is important in Hungary too. Béla Bartók was one of Hungary's greatest **composers**. He blended traditional folk music with classical music. Hungarian dance houses are found all over the country. There, people enjoy folk dances. Some dancers wear traditional costumes, including colorful skirts that spread out as dancers spin around.

FACT!
Hungary celebrates its 1848 revolution against Austria on March 15.

This Hungarian artist paints at a market in Budapest.

Christmas and Easter are the most important holidays in Hungary. Hungarians also celebrate Saint Nicholas Day on December 6. Children leave their shoes out the night before. In the morning, the shoes are filled with treats. It's a fun tradition!

People celebrate Easter in this Hungarian village by playing with water!

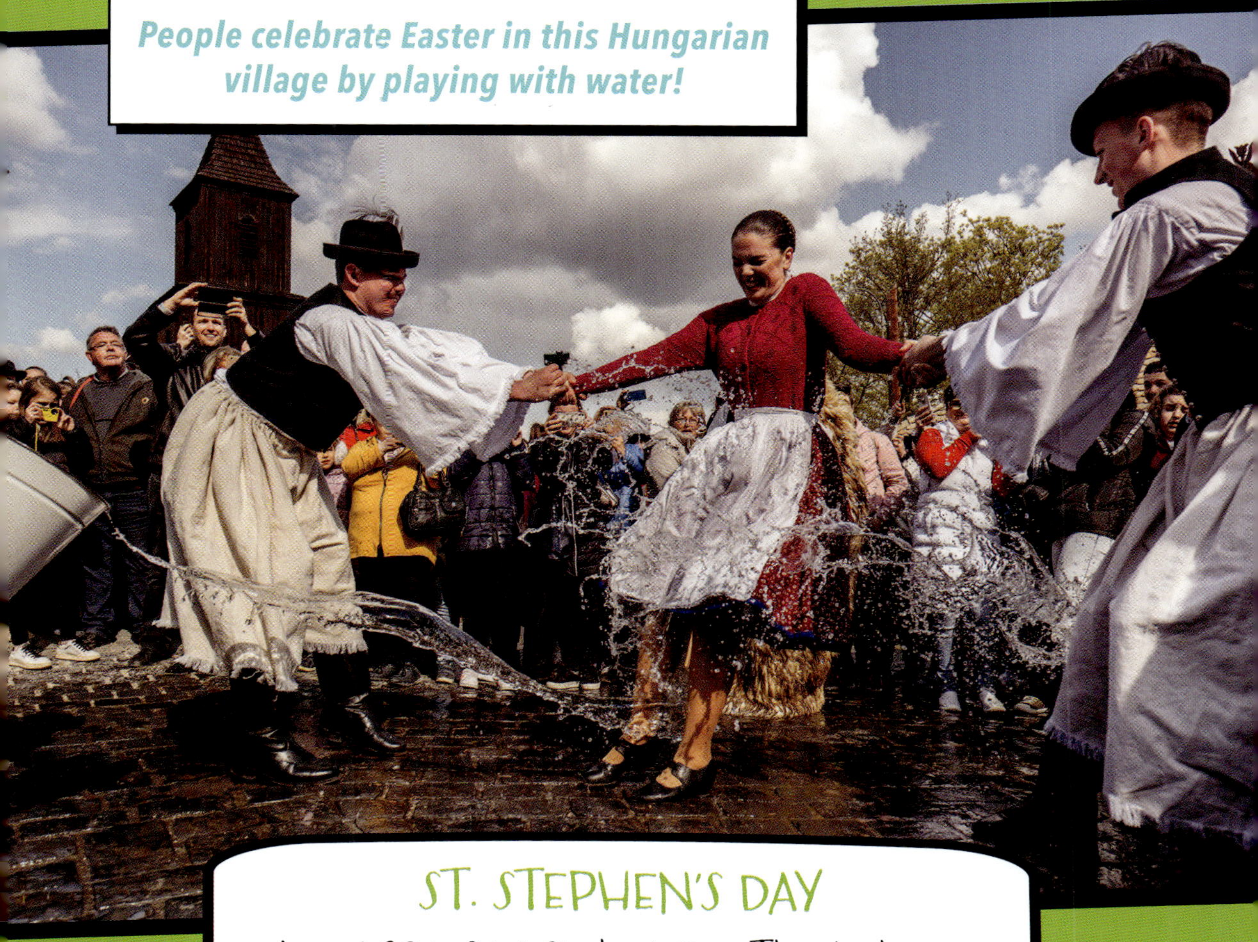

ST. STEPHEN'S DAY

August 20 is Saint Stephen's Day. This day honors Hungary's first king. There are always lots of fireworks!

FUN AND PLAY

Hungary has many pastimes for people to enjoy. Hungarian families and friends enjoy spending time together. They visit museums and parks. They go out to eat and attend concerts, movies, and plays. They relax in public spas, such as the Szechenyi Baths in Budapest.

WATER SPORTS

Many Hungarians enjoy water sports such as swimming and water polo. One reason water sports are so popular is the thermal springs that allow people to enjoy the water for much of the year.

Many people enjoy swimming, boating, and fishing on Lake Balaton.

People in Hungary enjoy many different sports. Soccer is the most popular. People also enjoy riding bikes. The country has almost 1,400 miles (2,253 km) of trails. Other popular activities include hiking and horseback riding.

Hungarians have won gold medals at many Summer Olympic Games. Some of their best Olympic sports are fencing and swimming. Hungary has won more gold medals in men's water polo than any other country in the Olympics!

FACT!

As of 2024, Hungary has won 189 gold medals in the Olympics.

Hungarian sculptor and designer Ernő Rubik was interested in creating geometric models. He invented the famous Rubik's Cube puzzle!

FOOD

Hungary is known for its hearty, sometimes spicy, foods. Hungarians eat a rich stew called goulash. Goulash may be a mix of things including beef, potatoes, tomatoes, peppers, and onions.

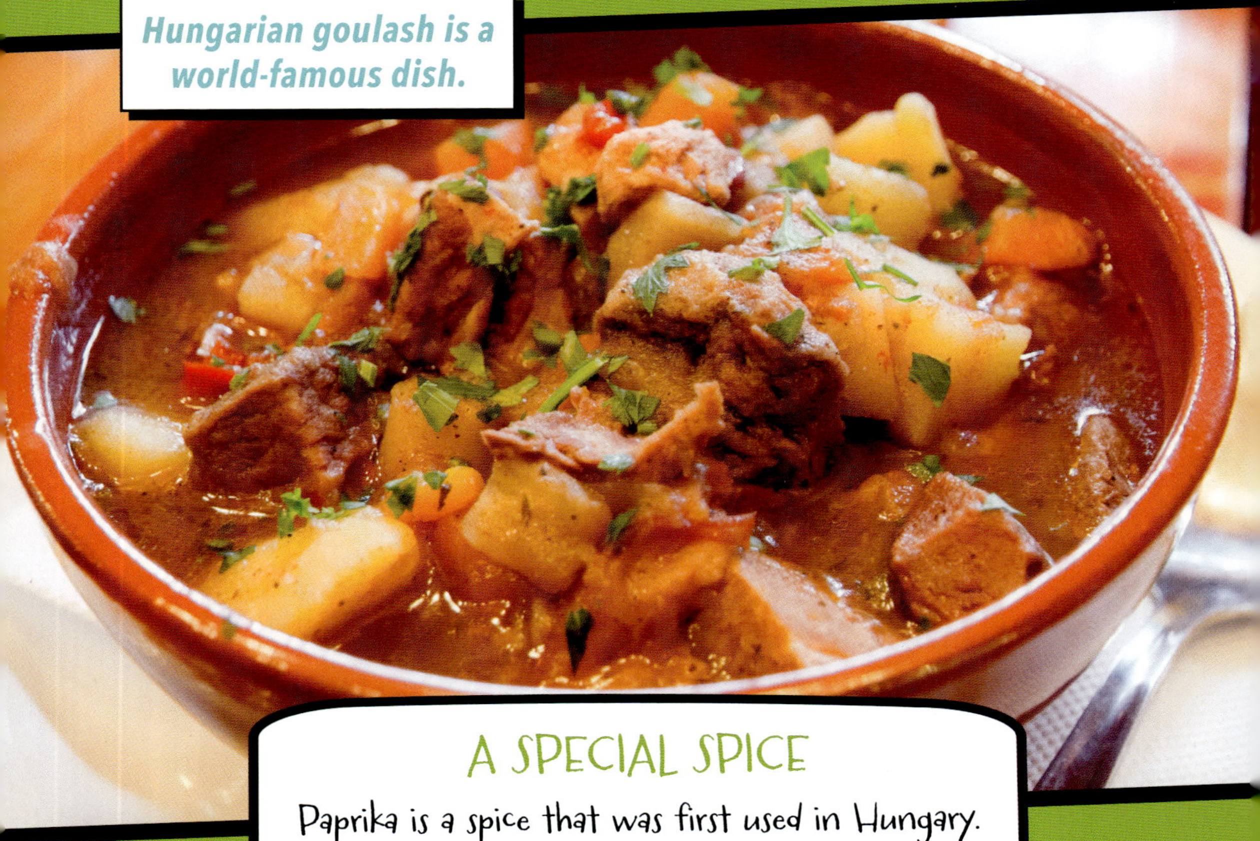

Hungarian goulash is a world-famous dish.

A SPECIAL SPICE

Paprika is a spice that was first used in Hungary. This powder made of red peppers is used in many foods, such as goulash.

Hungarians enjoy beef and chicken dishes. Meat is often served with noodles or dumplings. Cabbage leaves and peppers can be stuffed with meat or rice to create a filling and tasty meal. Sausages and kebabs of grilled meat and vegetables are popular street foods. *Langos* is another popular street food. It is a fried dough that is topped with sour cream and cheese.

Hungarians also like sweets. They may enjoy cakes made of apples and walnuts. Kiffles are a popular cookie often eaten on holidays. These cookies are filled with fruit jam and topped with powdered sugar.

FACT!

Paprikash is a chicken stew with a lot of paprika and sour cream.

Pancakes called palacsinta are filled with fruit and nuts. This one is served with plum jam.

GLOSSARY

architecture: The art or science of building; types of buildings.

Communist: Relating to a type of government where all property is owned by the state.

composer: A person who writes music.

culture: The beliefs and ways of life of a certain group of people.

diverse: Having many different parts.

ethnic: Related to people who have a common national or cultural tradition.

fossil fuel: A fuel, such as coal, oil, or natural gas, formed in the earth over millions of years from plant or animal remains.

Holocaust: The killing of European civilians and especially Jews by the Nazis during World War II.

ornate: Full of decoration.

thermal: Of, relating to, or caused by heat.

tourism: The business of drawing in tourists, or people traveling to visit another place.

tradition: A way of thinking, behaving, or doing something that's been used by people in a particular society for a long time.

violence: The use of force to harm others.

FIND OUT MORE

Books

Aradhya, Kerry. *Ernő Rubik and his Magic Cube*. Atlanta, GA: Peachtree, 2024.

Klepeis, Alicia. *Hungary*. Minneapolis, MN: Bellwether Media, 2023.

Spanier, Kristine. *Hungary*. Minneapolis, MN: Pogo Books, 2022.

Websites

Hungary
kids.britannica.com/kids/article/Hungary/345705
Learn more about Hungary, including its rich past and its biodiversity.

Hungary Factss
www.kids-world-travel-guide.com/hungary-facts.html
Check out these fun facts about Hungary, chosen by kids like you.

Video

Travel To Budapest: City Exploring for Kids
www.youtube.com/watch?v=o3ahE8G-bYM
Take a virtual tour of Budapest with The Touring Teacher.

INDEX